SKY COUNTRY

SKY COUNTRY

poems by

CHRISTINE KITANO

AMERICAN POETS CONTINUUM SERIES, NO. 162

BOA EDITIONS, LTD. ⸺ ROCHESTER, NY ⸺ 2017

Copyright © 2017 by Christine Kitano
All rights reserved
Manufactured in the United States of America

First Edition

For information about permission to reuse any material from this book, please contact The Permissions Company at www.permissionscompany.com or e-mail permdude@gmail.com.

Publications by BOA Editions, Ltd.—a not-for-profit corporation under section 501 (c) (3) of the United States Internal Revenue Code—are made possible with funds from a variety of sources, including public funds from the Literature Program of the National Endowment for the Arts; the New York State Council on the Arts, a state agency; and the County of Monroe, NY. Private funding sources include the Lannan Foundation for support of the Lannan Translations Selection Series; the Max and Marian Farash Charitable Foundation; the Mary S. Mulligan Charitable Trust; the Rochester Area Community Foundation; the Steeple-Jack Fund; the Ames-Amzalak Memorial Trust in memory of Henry Ames, Semon Amzalak, and Dan Amzalak; and contributions from many individuals nationwide. See Colophon on page 80 for special individual acknowledgments.

Cover Art: *Hallelujah: The Floating Mountain* by Michael Yamashita
Cover Design: Sandy Knight
Interior Design and Composition: Richard Foerster

BOA Logo: Mirko

Library of Congress Cataloging-in-Publication Data

Names: Kitano, Christine, 1985- author.
Title: Sky country / Christine Kitano.
Description: First edition. | Rochester, NY : BOA Editions Ltd., [2017] |
  Series: American poets continuum ; no. 162
Identifiers: LCCN 2017012292 (print) | LCCN 2017018707 (ebook) | ISBN
  9781942683445 (eBook) | ISBN 9781942683438 (softcover)
Subjects: LCSH: Japanese Americans—Poetry. | BISAC: POETRY / American /
  Asian American. | HISTORY / Asia / Korea.
Classification: LCC PS3611.I8775 (ebook) | LCC PS3611.I8775 A6 2017 (print)
  |
  DDC 811/.6—dc23
LC record available at https://lccn.loc.gov/2017012292

BOA Editions, Ltd.
250 North Goodman Street, Suite 306
Rochester, NY 14607
www.boaeditions.org
A. Poulin, Jr., Founder (1938–1996)

For my mother and father,
okage sama de

Contents

—∿∿—

A Leaving

after a poem by Wisława Szymborska

Some country is changing
shape, these people fleeing

those people. It is difficult
to name what these people

leave behind. They might open
closets and dresser drawers

but then close them: the wool
coat, so long saved-for, too

bulky, the lace underwear still
wrapped in tissue. They might

carry bundles on their backs,
or bags in both hands. Or,

they carry children, wailing
infants swaddled in cotton,

runny-nosed toddlers who
would otherwise fall behind.

By sunset, they walk or run
in orderly rows. Their path

barely lit. The sky a slate on which
no stars dare write a name.

I

Sky Country

The Korean word for heaven is *ha-neul nara*, a kenning that translates literally to "sky country." It was a word often used by potential immigrants to describe the United States.

I.

My grandmother hoards gold dollar-coins, the heavy discs etched with Sacagawea's over-the-shoulder glance, an infant son tied in a blanket to her back. She doesn't know who Sacagawea is, or Lewis and Clark, or figures from most stories we read in elementary school. Instead, the Bible and Hollywood sculpt her history. Over dinner she'll re-enact the events in *The Ten Commandments*: she raises her arms, as if in victory, to summon the Pillar of Fire and split the Red Sea, her small hands pushing apart two walls of water so that Charlton Heston can arrive safely on the bank. "Yes," she'll nod, soup dripping from her chin. "That's exactly how it happened."

2.

My Korean is weak. I understand only pieces of what she says. But from her cycle of stories, familiar nouns and images emerge. 1953: Pregnant with my mother, my grandmother flees south, my aunt strapped to her back. (At this point, my aunt will point to her bowed legs, the calves that curve outward below the knees, as evidence of this journey.) There is always a boat, a river, and a fire. My grandmother runs toward one and away from another but someone, perhaps my grandfather, grabs her hand to pull her back. I don't know why. There are men, Korean men and American men. She tells them her name, or that she's pregnant, but I never understand how or if they respond. Often, the stories end with her turning around to find her husband has vanished.

3.

Heaven. Sky Country. In America, the streets overflow with milk and honey.

For stealing day-old donuts, my mother is fired from her first American job, cleaning offices in a downtown Los Angeles high-rise.

Still, this is America. America is good, she says. You don't know how good you have it here.

4.

I return to Los Angeles for New Year's. My grandmother asks where I live now and tries to pronounce the words: *New York*. Is it hot or cold there, she asks. Is there Korean food? Is there a church? She asks if New York is where President Bush lives, then what will happen if America loses the war. Would I raise the Iraqi flag, give up English for Arabic? I want to tell her it's not that kind of war, but I don't have the words. She cackles. "You don't know," she says.

5.

My grandmother speaks Korean but, a child of colonial Korea, reads and writes in Japanese. Now, of course, she conducts her life in English. She worries what I'll do with an English degree, not because of the "adjunct situation" or the overall decline of the humanities, but because she knows countries are not the concrete, black-outlined shapes that seem so permanent when we open our textbooks. She knows how history can wipe away a person's language. She's been the real civilian I can only try to imagine when I read articles in the newspaper over hot coffee.

It's my grandmother who ran, four months pregnant, five-year-old daughter clasped to her back. It's she who pleaded and begged, who prayed that a soldier would listen when she screamed her name. It's her home that was severed by an arbitrary line, her family, like a brittle branch, snapped down the middle.

6.

After the traditional dinner of dumpling soup, my grandmother calls me over, unzips the small pocket on her backpack. She takes out a wrinkled manila envelope. Inside are one hundred gold dollar-coins. She's been collecting all year, trading for them at the Mexican grocery and the Hollywood Park racetrack. I thank her, but tell her not to go through all the trouble, that they aren't worth more than paper money. She shrugs. "You don't know," she says.

II

Now regard what sort of shape
this constellation takes.
It sits there like a jagged scar,
massive, on the massive landscape.
It lies there like the rusted wire
of a twisted and remembered fence.

—Lawson Fusao Inada, "Concentration Constellation"

Gaman. A Japanese term meaning to endure, persist, persevere,
or to do one's best in times of frustration and adversity.

". . . the employment of **gaman** *by, for example, the Issei*
during World War II in order to endure the humiliation and
hardships of incarceration, is mistaken by many non-Japanese to
indicate a lack of assertiveness or initiative rather than strength
in the face of difficulty and suffering."

—*Encyclopedia of Japanese American History:*
An A-to-Z Reference from 1868 to the Present
Brian Niiya, ed.

Gaman

It was night when the buses stopped.
It was too dark to see the road,

or if there was a road. So we waited.
We watched. We thought of back home,

how the orchards would swell with fruit,
how the trees would strain, then give way

under their ripe weight. The pockmarked
moon the face of an apple, pitted

with rot. But of course not. Someone
would intervene, would make of our absence

a profit. When we came, the boat, anchored
at San Francisco Bay, swayed for hours . . .

the gauntlet of uniformed men so intent
on finding cause to turn us away. And now

again, we wait. We watch. Our American children
press against us with their small backs.

Which gives us pause. For the sake of the children,
we'll teach them to forgive the fears of others,

the offenses. But what we don't anticipate
is how the dust of the desert will clot our throats,

how much fear will conspire to keep us silent.
And how our children will read this silence

as shame. However much we tried, we thought,
to demonstrate grace. When the buses stopped,

it was too dark to see the road. Or if there was a road. It was night. And instead of speaking, we waited.

Instead of speaking, we watched.

February, 1943: Topaz Concentration Camp, Utah

after a poem by Tomas Tranströmer

In February, life stands still. The sky is empty,
endless blue. Like a boat leashed to a dock,
the body carves the same groove in the same
circle of water. The skeletal trees do not meet our gaze.

The mountains, too, are turned away. The snow's depth,
as if a miracle, remains unchanged. No one comes
to say hello, or good-bye. Trapped in their own
rhythm, cyclones of powdered snow wheel in and out

through the cracks. But one day, something
approaches the window. The children rustle
from the corners. The eye strains to see what color
blazes. For a moment, everything turns around.

Equinox

Blame the late storm.
Or blame the earth itself,
ice-stunned soil smothering
the torn green shoots.

Once we lived, but now:
an empty house, an empty
field, an orchard emptying
of fruit. At home so long,

then by dawn, we were gone.
This dawn: Utah's mountains
trimmed with a thin, purple
cold. But even this winter eases

into spring. Elsewhere,
water must rush forth.
Mist clears, leaves must
brighten to green. With

or without permission,
another season will pass.
The fence leans its shadow,
but for how long

can one stand against
what the natural world
springs toward?

I Will Explain Hope

But not today, not when the wind carries
only the voices of geese crying but sailing
far above our human heads. Down here
I'd swear I feel the earth's subtle tug
on its slow travel around a distant sun.
But I'd also believe time stopped within
this patch of desert. That, elsewhere, lives go on
making marked progress but we remain
stranded within a stalled circle, surrounded
by a light that fails and fails to reach us.
How far and fast it travels, this light
that is already dead. How far and fast
it must journey, the prayer whispered in the dark.
What choice but to forgive such a brave failure?

Fireflies

Because they have never seen anything like it,
the city children weave through the barracks calling us
to come see. Our stories of fireflies in Japan
must echo in their young heads, how we'd picnic
in summer heat to watch the lit bodies punctuate
the dark. Better than Christmas, we'd told them.
So when they pull us into the Utah night, how to tell them
these pulsing clouds are not fireflies, but moths. Still,
we chase them through the desert fields, the children
cupping small fists around moon-whitened wings
that collapse, not from the children's touch, but the sheer
pressure of air. My mother would say the fireflies
are the lights of soldiers killed in a war far away,
their spirits now wandering the earth in search of home.
But these are not fireflies. How to say fireflies
don't come to Utah, how to say how close, or far,
we are from home? How to say where we are
at all? My daughter catches one, its brief body torn,
and flickering in her palm. I teach her the word *hotaru*,
firefly. Together we trace the letters in the dirt
with our fingers. But the next morning, when she
peeks outside, she cries to find the characters gone,
the name on the earth already erased by the wind.

About the Trees

Here is the handful
of shadow I have brought back to you:
this decay, this hope, this mouth-
ful of dirt, this poetry.
—Margaret Atwood, "Mushrooms"

Somewhere in central Utah,
off the loneliest road in America,
grows a plot of scattered trees.

That first fall, men carved shrubs
from the surrounding mountains
and transplanted them around camp.

Sure they'd die, we were all
surprised when, in spring, knuckles
of green burst from the branches.

The soil was grainy, and soft
as sand. The trees were a miracle, as if
born from a handful of shadow.

Maybe "miracle" is too strong
a word. I once thought it easy
to believe a vivid memory

was all that mattered. But now,
sometimes I see the trunks skeletal
and bare, the branches hardened

to iron. Or, they're lush as evergreens
in winter. How much depends on how
we're willing to remember. Now,

I sleep in an air-conditioned room
and watch television long past
dark. And when they ask me

about camp, I sift through memories
for a funny anecdote. The food,
or the smell of the latrines . . .

This morning, I woke before dawn.
I stared at the clock's neon numbers,
my hands again full of shadows.

Believe me. The men were not angry.
But when they dug the trees from the earth,
anger bled through their hands.

The men returned with the trees
over their shoulders, the stunned roots aloft
and curled into incomplete fists.

III

Leaving California

Nothing has changed yet.
The moon fades, stars

recede into their star-shaped
pockets, and the sun, almost

early, swells the slots
between the California hills.

You'll go. Not today, but already
you know the ocean that tugs you

west, toward an unknown
home, the slow drawn

bow of this coast
subtle but taut, and waiting.

Before the Divorce, a Dry Thunderstorm

Though lightning sections the sky and thunder breaks,
then breaks again, rain will not come. I near the fence,
trash bag in hand, the narrow backyard expanse like the stage
for a school play after the children have long gone. I see
approaching what might be the shapes of horses, or the long,
wind-pressed shadows of trees. This, our shard
of the American dream: a house with a fence, the same
houses and fences on either side. The automatic
sprinklers sputter on, spitting fake rain across flattened
scabs of grass. Tonight, drought is abstraction, a hollow
phrase I cannot grasp. So too is divorce, how we will split
a house. It is small, the TV-lit window just one of many
in the dark, a neighborhood of boat-lights afloat
on what must be a finite sea. The pattern repeats: heat-
lightning, thunder, silence, the sky still stubborn with indigo
clouds. Rain will come, though probably not tonight.
I wait anyway. The thick air hovers just above me.

Ancestors

You'd like to imagine them at sea now,
having grown tired of haunting your sleep.
Perhaps they've held their words so long
they can now breathe underwater, their feet
webbed, their bodies edged with ocean-lace.
On your way to the fields you call to them,
and sometimes, they call back. You pray
they can see the sky above the water's surface,
and that they forgive the ocean, the field
upon field of space, the exact
span of a daughter's disobedience.

Lucky Come Hawai‘i

> Why settle for 35 cents a day
> Stripping cane
> When I can sleep with a Chinaman
> And make a dollar?
> —Translation of a Japanese field song

When night arrives in camp, you offer the men
your white body: their callused hands root

through the humid dark for flesh untouched
by sun. They crave your breath, your cool hands

smooth as abalone shell, your fine feet
two slim canoes. While their wives sleep,

blistered from stripping cane in the sun
swathed fields, robes slip with a shiver

from your slender shoulders. Shoulders like
slices of white melon from back home, your cheeks

the pink blossoms from their childhood trees.
Lucky come, they say, lucky come

Hawai‘i, Honolulu, Waialua, but the new vowel-thick
names hollow when you say them aloud. You know better,

that this hissing is not rain, but rats rustling the clustered
hearts of the banyan trees. Waves rise and break,

the rush of water like the sound of a skirt
gathering in a fist.

Summer: Insomniac Stages Her Love

Curtain: daylight, follow-spot on skin, blue
mottled where unmanned grief spreads her bruise.

Cue fog, enter lover, under whose touch I unravel
like black silk, whose fingers loosen the ache

nestled in my bones. In this light my body swells
with a summer of lust previously unknown. Take

me in, love. Forgive me my sins, love, I'm
yours: pleasure, privilege, and song.

But now, curtain. Lights down. Next scene.
Who finds comfort in sleep? Who pursues

that deeper urge? The moon in its crayon outline
shakes and glows. The cues are marked—warning,

standby, go. From here on I'll hold my own.
I can almost see your whole body in the dark.

Monologue of the Dental Assistant

My daughter lives in Arizona
with her father, I confess to patients
who listen without choice, waiting—
gums cottoned, jaws loosening—
for anesthesia to numb them whole.
Texas plains stretch, then disappear
outside the office window. But we talk
every night on the phone, I assure them,
then nudge a plastic straw beneath
a cheek flap to suck out their spit.

The kind ones look at me, their eyes
meet mine over my surgical mask,
but others drift away, their eyes rolling
instead toward the monitor to stare
at their own x-rays. They all
look the same—black and white
pockets of fog, gray tangles of tendons.
The doctor will be in soon, I say.
In fourth grade, at nine, the age
my daughter is now, we dissected squids
for science, donned paper masks,
shower caps, powdery latex gloves
with their rubber-band snap. Practice
for my adult future—I would be a surgeon,
a wife, a mother. So when I peeled
apart that sliced gelatinous squid to reveal
yolk-yellow sacs, I felt sure I was special,
that the teacher had chosen me.
Of course she hadn't. But I think of this
when I part a patient's lips to find
two even rows of teeth, snug in pink gums
as eggs in their cardboard cartons.

Driving home after work through purple
dusk, I pass the fairgrounds, the lights
from the Ferris wheel blinking in poor
approximations of stars. My daughter
called to say she needs a training bra, that
her father brought home some lacy thing
from a mall store. Her voice, a nameless
emotion that fills me over, and I can answer
as her mother, as his ex-wife, as Shawna
your dental assistant, but not as me.

Insomniac in Winter

after a poem by Anna Swir

Your breaths slow and multiply, each one
thickening the space between us. And with no air
of privilege, you fall easily into sleep. Do you not
see that death stands over our bed, the lidless eyes

that stare through you as if through a window?
My warm woman, under our bed a reservoir widens.
Past midnight, thunder shakes me again to life.
Can I pull you back to wrap myself in your simple heat,

will you steady me with your living hands?
No. Already, your heavy dreams nudge me aside.
I cannot join you, you simple fool, you
who dares leave, who dares sleep.

Monologue of the Fat Girl

"That is how they would remember her: a girl whose hapless body was destined to be fat."
—Andre Dubus, "The Fat Girl"

It wasn't always like this—
at nine, my bathing suit
stuck to the hollows
in my chest, my ribs
were distinct as fish gills.
At summer camp,
I taught the younger girls
to swim—they roped
their fragile arms
around my neck, then
squealed as I dove
into the wide blue lake.

But now, night emerges
with its thick tablecloth,
the pregnant moon a tilted
cup of milk.
The doctors say to eat
before the pang strikes,
the ache that calls forth
the white room whose door
I can't seem to shut.
Instead, I sink
into a hot bath, allow
the water to rise
over the hills of my body—
the tide closes in
on the tender peaks
of my breasts and it is only
here I can breathe, finally,
underwater. I know
what my husband hopes

when he circles or crosses out
dates on the bedside calendar.
He hopes also for a boy,
but mostly that all this
adds up to something.
My underwear's elastic
has left its imprint,
a row of shark teeth
belted around my waist.

That summer at camp,
I prepared the buckets
of tie-dye ink, unscrewed
the medicine-drop bottles
and watched the ink blossom
in water—red, yellow, blue—
the colors spilling into each other,
expanding but weightless,
and without shape.

Pink steam rises,
almost pulsing in the bath
light. My husband
is still out. A knot
inside slackens, and I feel it
before I see the red
unspool like loosed
silk, the familiar blood
dilating in the bathwater,
the unraveling ribbon
of a spine.

Insomniac in Spring

Let me say it how we've been taught
to say it: I love you. Or, I miss you.
These words that fail their meanings.

Spring here, it's as if last night's rain
pricked a green vein, our tree
this morning steeped in color.

In your absence, I cannot still your figure
in my mind, your face an inkblot refusing
a shape. Spring insists on love but clouds

froth in the sky's steel cauldron.
The lawn may appear lush as velvet
but up close it's all weed, water-grass.

Somewhere near, a house or animal
burns. For all I know, you're gone
for good. But I hold out. Shadow puppets

rehearse their perfect choreography
in my heart. I can't help it.
I have no words.

Choose Your Own Adventure: Go South

Under a rusted water fountain
at a rest stop in Pennsylvania, you find a small jar
filled with a woven cocoon, or perhaps

the mummified remains of a rat. Birth or death,
you take it, secure it in the cup holder then drive
the day, the glass rattling—no, trembling—

within its plastic restraints. At sunset, a translucent
honey-gold fills the car, and the trees in what is now
Virginia lean in close. The elms are large as clouds.

In the motel that night, unclothed, you slip
into the indoor pool. It is heated, and lit from below
like a cauldron. You don't know how to swim,

so you float, the glowing water buoys you up. In that
sulfurous light, with your arms spread like wings,
you might be an airplane's x-shaped shadow

or a child's summertime toy. But soon, your body
collapses like a broken ruler and water fills your nose,
the tile walls suddenly snug. Always the way we notice

change, the space around us almost the same,
then not. Same, same, but different, like the moment
the elevator door finally slides shut.

You wake the next morning in the motel bed,
hair still wet. Your neck aches. Someone had curled
you up like a small animal, someone had placed

the jar on the nightstand beside you, its contents
now vanished. Or simply emptied. From your head,
a chlorinated map seeps onto the sheets.

Confess that you're sorry. Confess that you're not.
The transparent jar glimmers in the dusty half-light.
You continue south.

Insomniac in Fall

Red leaves spread their fever through the trees
and tonight, for the first time,

I lie down alone. Aloneness the body's own
medication. I will not notice that your absence

enlarges the bedroom walls, or how
the window allows in the large autumn air.

If I prayed, I'd pray: let me leave you, let you
leave me. Tonight I lie, as an animal

should, alone. Tonight I fill my head
with thoughts that do not contain you.

Tonight I ignore the stars that congregate
in a shrug. Tonight I will remember

I sleep, as we all always do, alone.

Worship

The men set fire to the fields.
Flames erupt above the plants,
the canes' casings and leaves crumple
to ash, revealing the tender
stalks where the sugar sleeps.
Do we always know where value lies?
Fire season. They've been feeding
the flames all night. At dawn,
when the particulate wind rips
through the purple smoke, I find myself
hurled, still enthralled, into the volcanic light.
Despite the fire, the surrounding world remains
silent as an altar. The rain of charred leaves
soft, like the molt of a still breathing beast.

Insomniac Starts an Exercise Routine

The first week passes, then two. Soon, it has already been six months. A mile's distance feels less slog, more flight. Her body in flux, when she reaches behind to scratch a shoulder blade, she feels a thickness, a heft where before had been just bone. New swellings rise—not tumors, as first feared—but muscles, the names of which she has to look up in a textbook: *latissimus dorsi, biceps brachii, vastus lateralis,* the words long and Latin, like the names of stars. Others comment on the angles now articulated in her face. But it isn't, as they say, the shedding of an old layer. And it isn't, as has been said, the angel emerging from its stone. The end product will be a complete transformation: total, and final. Beneath her skin, a new form pieces itself together. The bruises that speckle her limbs bud from within. One day, as if waking from a dream, she'll find a new face in place of the old. Perhaps with gills etched behind her ears. Maybe fins in place of feet. Or instead of arms: wings.

IV

Years Later, Washing Dishes, A Vision

after a poem by Robert Wrigley

Dawn at the kitchen sink, sunrise still
climbing across the California hills,
the jacaranda's shaking: an invisible hand
rocks the yellow porch swing, lifts and unfurls
the tarp awning to startle dozens of house sparrows,
their flight sudden and erratic. Beyond
the loosening leaves, my father, as if returning
from fetching the mail, rises through it all,
the leaves and the mist, his hands (smaller now,
it seems) clutched in front of him, as if holding
a letter only he can see. Water overflows
the open bowl of my hands.

The Night Before Your 28ᵗʰ Birthday

You no longer dream your dead father alive in your childhood home. You're an adult now, at least five studio apartments removed from that archetypal v-roofed house, curlicues of smoke rising from the rectangle chimney. So instead, the house you now live in sprouts a flight of stairs down which your father descends, holding a lit birthday cake. At least you believe it him, though the skeptic in you nudges your ribs: has he really come this long way just to sit with you on the porch the night before your birthday? Mosquitoes circle the dying streetlamp, the light flickers on and off, then on again. Of course he is tired, so he holds his hands, palms upturned, on his knees. He wears khakis. His breath effortless, his stroke-broken eye still the color of milk, but almost starry now. Can he see? You ask, but he says it is better to forget what is no longer relevant. And that's exactly how he says it: *no longer relevant.* Though he's only an arm's length away, his voice is a distant wax-paper voice. "Blow out the damn candles," he says, "I don't have all night." Around you, the neighborhood flattens to an empty field. Though you know this is a dream, you make the wish. For one breathless moment, you believe.

Roofing

for Brooks Haxton

June. School now out,
the agapanthus edges
toward bloom—clusters
of slim stars, spattered
blue and purple
down narrow throats.
Noon. My father's
stayed home to patch
the roof. I wait
by the ladder, pinch
new buds from stems,
but the feeble petals wilt
in my hand. With each
step the roof groans,
the air flushed
with the dust of red
gravel. I taste
tar, hot and bitter
on the back of my tongue.
I can't see him
from where I stand,
though I imagine
his profile, hunched
against the sun.
The flowers' dark ink
floods the fortune-lines
of my palm. I'm sure
he's going to fall
right through.

Bring in the Flowers Before the Santa Anas

after a line by Gary Young

Invisible fires surround this house so the sky,
reading our thoughts as always, grows still—
despite the thicket of air, fat clouds muscle for room.
Soon they will smudge out the sun.

The first gust swings wind chimes in muted light.
Discordant tones ring against the backdrop
of a neighbor's windows slamming shut. Sudden,
like the ears of a small animal, the petals
of a long-necked orchid shiver at my ankle.

Like flecks of black snow, ash floats, soundless.
Behind me: the rustle of paper, the shuffle of slippers,
or a water kettle's tremolo. It is not yet time,
but someone knows, already, to call me back.
I shake dust from my skirt, wipe ash from my face.
Someone is crying my name.

Autobiography of the Poet at Sixteen

My father in his last year,
        half-blind and craving salt
                air, out the window

leans, face pushed into a beam
        of sun, and can't see
                me, down the street, that I've

skipped school again, ceding
        instead to the coastline,
                to the edge where the shore

shoulders sea. What is it I felt?
        I can say it now: guilt that swells
                the space between my ribs,

guilt that fills my throat
        when I parcel out
                twelve pills from his medicine

drawer, enough I hope
        to stop cold
                this sixteen-year-old's weak

heart. California winter,
        the beach almost quiet, almost
                still, the pier's carnival music

trickles through the waves
        that make the same wave-
                sounds again and again,

and again. I vomit out of sheer
        fear, the individual pills
                surface and spill, almost

intact, onto the packed sand.
        What now? The memory fades then.
                Not until years later do I suspect

we are built for life,
        for love, which means
                we are built for pain.

But my sixteen-year-old self
        refuses to allow even a simple
                sadness, the hint instead

burrowed deep in my gut that knows
        all that I know now
                but couldn't know then.

A Story with No Moral

Los Angeles, 1989

My mother and I are fighting again over what I should wear. I'm
small, maybe four years old. I don't remember why I don't want to
wear what she picks out, but recall a sense of general discomfort—
stockings that bunch and won't stay up, nickel-sized buttons that
catch my hair, lace collars that itch around my neck. I pout. My
mother says nothing for a moment, then reaches into the closet
and yanks, in one surprisingly swift motion, a pink dress from its
hanger. She grips a ruffled sleeve in each hand, then pulls. The
dress rips down the bib, the pink cloth shredding, thin wisps of
pale thread framing the rupture. I'm scared. I know I'm not the
daughter my mother wants, but I still don't know who or what she
wants me to be.

South Korea, 1958

It isn't that my mother's family is poor, but that there is nothing to buy. American goods can be bribed from soldiers, but my mother has no one to barter on her behalf.

My grandmother's concerns are elsewhere. In the newly partitioned country, she's obsessed with claiming land. Her eyes scan the empty spaces left behind by war and she envisions buildings—storefronts, apartments, or hotels. In the torn fields behind her house, she crouches down to grip the soil in her hands.

My mother craves the little objects that money or care can buy: a toy kitchen set, a banana, a can of Del Monte peaches in sweet syrup. She sits in her school desk, tugging at the coarse wool stockings that my grandmother buys cheap in bulk. The winter outside is bitter, my mother's exposed face raw from the cold. A classmate slides into the seat beside her and reveals in her mittened palm American lip balm in a round tube. How miraculous that such a thing even exists.

Los Angeles, 1990

In kindergarten I befriend a girl named Lauren, one of the few girls in class who is smaller than me. My mother likes Lauren, calls her "little Barbie." Lauren's mother was once Miss Florida. My mother tells me, "Lauren's mom only wears ironed jeans." I'm not sure what this is supposed to indicate, but I nod and try to imitate the look of awe on my mother's face.

Lauren and I spend hours together after school dressing up in her old Halloween costumes. We pose in front of the sliding door mirrors. She's completely absorbed in her own image. And so am I. Her hair is a buttery blond, fluffy and soft, always tied back neatly in a bow. My mother tries to arrange my hair the same way but, too thin and stringy, it'll slip from her grasp. It puzzles me that this angers her.

This afternoon, Lauren's dressed as a mermaid. I help her tie the strings of a metallic purple bathing suit top, trying not to catch her hair. The glittering emerald tail cascades from her hips, and she drapes a shimmering gold scarf around her narrow shoulders. We're going to the ball, she announces. She's radiant. I don't remember what I'm wearing. In the mirror, I see Lauren's reflection and, despite the elaborate costume, think yes, that's Lauren. I look at the girl standing next to her, the reflection split where the two slides of mirror overlap, am almost unable to recognize myself.

South Korea, 1959

One of my mother's classmates is the daughter of a Korean woman and a black American soldier. The girl never speaks.

After school, my mother follows the girl to the lake. The girl plunges her naked body into the water. At first my mother thinks she is playing, but the girl, half submerged, scratches at her skin with her hands, then a branch, then a rock. My mother hides in the reeds.

Los Angeles, 1990

When I confess to my mother that I feel "ugly," she again tells me the
story of her classmate.

      What happened next, I ask.

      When the scabs peeled off, they left tight, polished scars.

      I ask what the moral of the story is.

      There is no moral, she says.

Friday Night Affair

". . . it's no wonder we pay to sit in the movie theatre so fear can jolt us and make our bodies lighter . . ."
—Christopher Kennedy, "No Wonder"

When the lights dim, I think again
of my father, how now, even in dreams,
he moves away from me, sliding behind
a wooden shutter, or always two steps ahead
on a worn path. I forget more than I remember,
unable to recall the shape of his wristwatch,
the size of his shoes, the precise curvature
of his swimmer's shoulders. I know that illness
weights the body even if the eyes
gaze skyward, that death tastes of salt,
heavy and cold. But I know, too,
that longing can lighten this load. Love
narrows the field of view so I can see
only what I want to see. When I slip
my hand into yours, I am weightless.

V

1942: In Response to Executive Order 9066,
My Father, Sixteen, Takes

No spare underwear.
No clean shirts, pants, or good shoes.
Instead, a suitcase
of records. His trombone.
This is not the whole story,
and yet, it is true.
It is a story without an ending.
And when I open my mouth
to speak, it continues.

Grandmother Tells Me a Story: Passing the Lake, Korea 1952

All day the lake is still, its breadth
unchanged though we have been walking

all afternoon. We balance cinched bundles
on our heads. (Like clouds, I imagine, though

of course they are not.) Up ahead, an old woman
falls out of line, hands her cloth-soled shoes to another,

then enters the water, breaking its stiff skin.
Her skirt blossoms around her lowering

head, a darkening halo. (No, I protest, but the story
continues): No one breaks ranks. The lake,

but for a skim of bubbles, unchanged.
(Or so my grandmother swears. Her metaphors

and my poor Korean commingle into myth). Above,
though stars crowd the heavens, only a dim light.

Chicken Soup

My grandmother pours salt
         into my right palm, places thin slivers
                  of garlic in my left. She explains

something about blood, how to salt
         the raw bird to drain its fluids,
                  but my mind already wanders:

I watch the chicken shrivel but compose
         instead the grandfather I've only met
                  in story: daybreak, he's just finished

mopping up in the buildings
         that sculpt this city's skyline, but it's
                  someone else's view of Los Angeles.

The immigrant sees, not the postcard-perfect lights,
         but the scuffed tiles, dust-lined desks, the darkening
                  throats of toilet after toilet.

Home, he tiptoes upstairs not to wake
         his daughters, holding his shoes
                  like a thief. He's fired

for stealing a roll of toilet paper, a can of soda
         for my mother. Children are nothing
                  but trouble, my grandmother says,

shaking a wooden spoon. My mother claims
         the story otherwise: it was she
                  who accompanied father to work, she

who stole a box of stale donuts, she
         who lost the family's first job. Grandmother
                  shrugs and repeats the same

conclusion. Never have children, she says,
      though her expression is hidden
            by the steam now rising from the pot.

It's a simple recipe: boil until the meat
      falls from the bones, easy, like a girl
            shedding a summer dress.

Last night, I cooked for friends.
      After dinner, my friend handed me
            his one-month son, who only

blinked when I nudged my thumb
      into his fist. Earlier, washing the pale
            bird, I struggled to keep the body

from slipping through my hands: I held
      its small-fleshed form under cold water,
            pulled the giblets out the round hollow

between its ribs and was surprised
      to be surprised when it didn't
            make a sound.

Persimmons

My mother calls them *gahm*,
savoring the round vowel.

When she pares off the skins,
they fall away like strips of ribbon.

Clusters of firm, waxy planets
slung low on a strained branch,

the tree a sudden stab of color
on the drab East L.A. corner.

The box arrives in fall, white
postal service cardboard wet

in the corners where the fruits
have already spilled their juice.

Faced with the open box, I think
my mother's word, but aloud exclaim

"persimmons." Persimmons,
the word in the only language I own.

Earthquake Drills

Have a plan.
Under your bed,

hard-soled shoes,
a flashlight, water

bottles, canned corn
niblets, peaches in sweet

syrup. San Andreas:
a mean line on a map.

How long until your earth
unzips itself? How long

for the fault to burst
its crooked seam?

For small comfort, count
bandages, replace batteries,

pack a bag, but admit
this: there is never a plan.

Instead: in deep night,
darkness thick on the lawn,

find your flashlight.
With your thumb,

click the switch. Watch
the sure light flicker on.

For the Korean Grandmother on Sunset Boulevard

So you are here. Night comes as it does
elsewhere: light pulls slowly away
from telephone posts, shadows of buildings
darken the pavement like something
spilled. Even the broken moon
seems to turn its face.
And again you find yourself
on this dark riverbed, this asphalt
miracle, holding your end of a rope
that goes slack when you tug it.
Such grief you bear alone.
But wait. Just now a light
approaches, its rich band draws
you forward, out of shadow.
It is here, the bus that will ferry
you home. Go ahead,
grandmother, go on.

Acknowledgments

Grateful acknowledgment is made to the editors of the following journals in which these poems or earlier versions of them appeared.

The Asian American Literary Review: "About the Trees," "For the Korean Grandmother on Sunset Boulevard," "*Gaman*";
Atticus Review: "Before the Divorce, a Dry Thunderstorm";
Blue Lyra Review: "Equinox," "Chicken Soup";
Chicago Quarterly Review: "Friday Night Affair," "Years Later, Washing Dishes, A Vision";
Codex Journal: "A Leaving";
Connotation Press: An Online Artifact: "Earthquake Drills";
Crab Orchard Review: "A Story with No Moral," "Lucky Come Hawai'i";
The Evansville Review: "Persimmons," "Worship";
Luna Luna Magazine: "Ancestors";
Miramar: "Bring in the Flowers Before the Santa Anas," "Roofing," "Fireflies," "Sky Country";
Newfound Journal: "Choose Your Own Adventure: Go South";
The Pinch: "The Night Before Your 28th Birthday";
Pinyon: "Monologue of the Dental Assistant";
Smartish Pace: "Grandmother Tells Me a Story: Passing the Lake, Korea, 1952";
Stringtown: "February, 1943: Topaz Concentration Camp, Utah";
Tar River Poetry: "Monologue of the Fat Girl";
Wildness: "Summer: Insomniac Stages Her Love," "Insomniac in Winter," "Insomniac in Spring," "Insomniac in Fall," "Insomniac Starts an Exercise Routine."

I would like to thank the Ithaca College Pre-Doctoral Diversity Fellowship and the Texas Tech University Dissertation Completion Fellowship for providing the time and space to complete this book. Thank you also to The Writer's Center in Bethesda, Maryland, for the Emerging Writer Fellowship. Thank you to Dr. Dennis Ogawa and the University of Hawai'i Manoa for their support.

For his unwavering support and guidance, my deepest gratitude to my poetry coach, Christopher Buckley.

At Texas Tech, thank you to Curtis Bauer, William Wenthe, Yuan Shu, and Jill Patterson. At BOA, thank you to Peter Conners, Jenna Fisher, Ron Martin-Dent, Kelly Hatton, and Sandy Knight. Thanks always to Brooks Haxton for teaching me how to use the word "and."

Thank you to Dean Leslie Lewis for bringing me to Ithaca College and thank you to my colleagues in the Writing and English departments for their friendship and support. Thanks especially to Tyrell Stewart-Harris, my comrade.

Thank you to my mother, Lynn, and my family.

Finally: thank you, Derek, for our big and noisy life.

About the Author

Christine Kitano is the author of *Birds of Paradise* (Lynx House Press). Born in Los Angeles to a Korean immigrant mother and a Japanese American father, she has lived in southern California, central New York, and west Texas. She earned her MFA at Syracuse University and her PhD at Texas Tech University. She teaches creative writing, poetry, and Asian American literature at Ithaca College.

BOA Editions, Ltd., American Poets Continuum Series

Colophon

BOA Editions, Ltd., a not-for-profit publisher of poetry and other literary works, fosters readership and appreciation of contemporary literature. By identifying, cultivating, and publishing both new and established poets and selecting authors of unique literary talent, BOA brings high-quality literature to the public. Support for this effort comes from the sale of its publications, grant funding, and private donations.

———

The publication of this book is made possible, in part, by the support of the following individuals:

Anonymous x 3
Nin Andrews
Angela Bonazinga & Catherine Lewis
Lauren D. Frank & Annette Miller
Gwen & Gary Conners
Gouvernet Arts Fund
Peg Heminway, *in honor of Grant Holcomb*
Sandi Henschel
Christopher Kennedy
X. J. & Dorothy M. Kennedy
Deborah Ronnen & Sherman Levey
Edith R. Matthai, *in memory of Peter Hursh*
Dan Meyers, *in honor of J. Shepard Skiff*
Nannette Nocon
Boo Poulin
Boo Poulin, *in honor of Sandi Henschel*
Steven O. Russell & Phyllis Rifkin-Russell
Sue Stewart, *in memory of Stephen L. Raymond*
Michael Waters & Mihaela Moscaliuc
Bernadette Weaver-Catalana

Printed in the USA
CPSIA information can be obtained
at www.ICGtesting.com
JSHW082224140824
68134JS00015B/730